playing the changes

Wesleyan Poetry

Also by Thulani Davis

All the Renegade Ghosts Rise

playing the changes

Thulani Davis

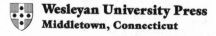 **Wesleyan University Press**
Middletown, Connecticut

To Shaku Joseph

Grateful acknowledgment is made to the following pub-
lications, in which the poems listed first appeared:
"being alone," *Elan*; "Backstage Drama," *The Village
Voice*.

Art: The New York Public Library Picture Collection,
Astor, Lenox and Tilden Foundations.

LIBRARY OF CONGRESS CATALOGING IN
PUBLICATION DATA

Davis, Thulani.
  Playing the changes.
  I. Title.
PS3554.A93779P55 1985 811'.54 84-10456
ISBN 0-8195-1120-X (alk. paper)
ISBN 0-8195-2119-1 (pbk.: alk. paper)

All inquiries and permissions requests should be ad-
dressed to the Publisher, Wesleyan University Press, 110
Mt. Vernon Street, Middletown, Connecticut 06457.

Distributed by Harper & Row Publishers, Keystone
Industrial Park, Scranton, Pennsylvania 18512.

Manufactured in the United States

First Edition

Wesleyan Poetry

Before coming to this book, these poems have been part of many performances in poetry and art spaces; installed with graffiti pens or hung on clothes and walls; warped and woofed through video synthesizers; danced and sung to music. I have been fortunate to have some collaborators in these projects who have taught and inspired me a great deal. I would especially like to thank Jessica Hagedorn, Ntozake Shange, Cecil Taylor, Anthony Davis, John Woo, Doris Chase, and my husband Joseph Jarman.

Jessica, June Jordan and Olga Broumas read this manuscript, talked to me, reread it, asked me questions, cared in detail. My friends have been family, my family, friends. Anything they can't handle goes to Bob Marley or Billie Holiday. God bless the child who knows she could be love and be loved. Thank you.

Thulani Davis
Summer 1984

contents

contessas and cardsharks

geography

skinny-dippin'

playing the changes

contessas and
cardsharks

contessas & cardsharks

slick boys and cardsharks,
baffled local prophets,
cane-colored contessas
with orange-black hair
crowd over a kitchen table.
professional elegants
out of work
they could hum you some Monk
or tell you about when Malcolm
was a child

black folks weren't supposed to be out
after dark or too much together
i only know what's left of it.
how Malcolm's daddy worked for Garvey
like some folks sweat for God.
But the midwest was an open
treacherous place,
full of leadbelly
and accidental death.
Where five or six blacks took hands
in small parlours with woodburning stoves
chanted 'Up Ye Mighty Race'
into the dreams of children tucked in.
a streetcar cut him in half.
he continued to live for hours
as word got out that his kind
were not needed in town.
we tell each other what we know.

people get offended.
a flotilla sits off the coast
of the revolution.
the Pope tells the priest
to mind his own business.
white hoods parade in Namibia,
rally round the kitchen window.

Malcolm's mother was from Grenada
followed the Black Star to Harlem.
we have what's left. just that.
romantic chroniclers gambling,
dabbling in dope,
experts in gruesome details.
white hoods, capering, silent
helicopters, reggae on the radio.

it's hard to stay in one piece.
ask Malcolm's daddy, Reverend Little.
ask those scrawling on walls.

is it a hairdo or are you Frankie Lymon?

we're not street kids anymore
it's just a look we have
don't even like the streets much now
they use you more than you use them
i'm still mad about what i was mad about
but no longer sad about
what i was sad about
i did what i could
& got what i got to be sad about now
i see we look so many ways
still givin' in to how we feel
we made that the oath
the code, the cool way to be
but there's more sex and death
than rock 'n' roll around here
we're not street kids anymore
it's just one of the looks we have
we're still hipper than the best
hang out like all the rest
but this is what comes after all that
we're not street kids anymore
it's just a look we have

he said he named the song "for you"
so he could play it in any town

kiss my neck
like petals of a peony fluttering
tell me how you love her
hold my hand
tell me how constant is truth
your mouth phrases her song
but you sing in my ear & beg a kiss
i tell you when & where
your voice is like dawn over mountains
the sea at my side rushing
rose over the hills
kiss my mouth
i lift your shirt
run petals down your chest
it's just that i'm jealous i say
but i love you too you say
oh yes, of course you do
sing it here
let your voice slip like sunlight
right here
now here

boppin' is safer than grindin'

i danced on "Shop Around"
but never the flip side
"Who's Lovin' You"
boppin' was safer than grindin'
(which is why you should not come around)

seein' you is a slow dance
that goes on too long
a formal i went to at 13
it ended in the middle of a kiss
so good we didn't hear the song end
until everyone laughed at us
alone on the dance floor
they wrapped us like a maypole
in streamers and scandal
he was somebody else's man
beware of slow dances & pretty men

boppin' is safer than grindin'
& somebody else's man / you remind me
this man i met livin' in a crowded house
he was so pretty all i could say was
oh wow when we had only the kitchen
for love will make you do foolish things
& oh wow when his kneecaps cracked
on the ceramic tile
as my head hit the dishwasher
i was in my world & i thought
beware of slow dances, pretty men,
& kitchen tile — (and you,
you should not keep comin' around)

your eyes make me reckless
& i might hurt myself
while the rest of you
makes me talk like this
to keep from sighin', cryin'
& going into narcissistic abandon

reminds me of this man
so fine all i could say was
death might be fun when i flew
off the bed / landed on my head
on the far wall nearly dead
i was in my world & i thought
good thing we're not head over heels
in love we might break something
in an act of vociferous desperation
singin' four-part harmonies
& Betty Carter's best lines
beware of slow dances, pretty men,
kitchen tile & fallin' out of bed

boppin' is safer than grindin'
& we cannot take a chance
not with your smile, your style
& the way we laugh in crowded houses
let's make a pact
not to bruise each other
or kiss each other with all we've got
cause boppin' is safer than grindin'
& i'd rather dance to "Shop Around"
than "Who's Lovin' You"

misogyny (1)

he lies with her
the berrybrown shaman
nestling himself like a deer
in rustling leaves
in minor chords
the night weeps
his harmony slips
from heartless lips
he comes to her bed to sleep

every night his breath
propels each leaf
fluttering across her skin
he sleeps   she dreams
fitful and electric
dreams of lips
wakes
then arms
then lips
wakes
like an animal
in a strange house

he comes to her bed
the shaman
for seven nights
undressing his ginger body
laying it upon her
rustling leaves
in her hair

he brushes like butterflies
by her ears
prying and plying
with promises
he speaks of living
without desire
but she knows

she has become
the most carnal woman
in the world

and he is so beautiful
she searches for flaws
then ceases to admit
he shares her bed
and only sees a man
who has no flesh

when finally he pulled her
to the pillows
she imagined
she fell

Ms. Oji's kimono

it is red
like a dress for Lady Day
or a blues for lonely women
it's a blood color frankly
a woman hue
for women of color
its edges are ragged / rough
it is thick and scarred
thick and scarred
standing up to lashes
admitting loss
thick and scarred
like my body
its scars regular
pyramids or tribal
land is carved this way
these scars are common earth
Ms. Oji's kimono is red
like Anna May's lips
tempting the West to fall
for lizard-eyed demons
monkey-faced warriors
menace when she rises
silent and leaves the room
Anna May's lips are red
like a dozen shirts in my closet
so i can be seen
she keeps her kimono in the kitchen
safe from thieves like me
who long to wear canvas and paint
like that

Roslyn

Roslyn has nothing going
nothing to fight for
no work to do
she couldn't name one desire
that is not someone else's
or a man

she cannot claim
where she came from
will not claim who she is
or the way she cries
so no one can see

she has no work to do
cannot finish books
feed herself
or go out alone
she is always late
not to sit alone somewhere
and wait
she wouldn't know what to do

Roslyn doesn't want a thing
but she waits for something anyway
she has no work to do
she holds off interests
passions and opinions
everything but the facts
and these come to her
from dramas and the papers

she agrees with fiction
and what people say
i wouldn't trust her in court
or on my back
a woman without a dream
is a fault in the earth
all steam and liquid fire

Roslyn goes to work
has a job
but no calling
waits for the word
to call herself
no one ever remembers her name
or where they saw her
she waits to be told
she's the only one

her tyranny is silent
small and sexual
her losses are great
she has not called herself
said, "I'm here, now, deal with me"

Roslyn wouldn't hurt a fly
but people fear her sleep
her unconscious
the primal whatever
that wants to play
it might have guns out
for the rest of us

misogyny (2)

They dressed like women and preferred to kiss men. They allowed themselves to remember embraces, not as they were but as they wished they were. They knew no women. Grown women were the reason, after all, that a good man needed a good man. Those women, they could not even remember, except in the tears of a sister left by a gambler or the tragic death of those loose and dangerous, like ever-present scandals there was always one. One queen whose hips were real; one high bitch who taught them all their tricks, whose thighs defined the night as they sliced her dress, whose breasts could be touched, whose desires murdered young men. The young boys with tender hearts. They loved her eyes more than she ever could. They dreamed of her death each night and dressed. One dressed as the virgin mary, one as a street-corner whore, and they tormented each other, trying the pledges of gothic novels against the penance of the church. They loved sin and dirt and low-down ladies and murdered themselves with the knives, chains, fists and broken glass of young boys' cock fights.

Bad Brains, a band

        the idea that they think must scare people to death
the only person i ever met from southeast DC
was genius who stabbed her boyfriend
for sneaking up on her in the kitchen
she was tone deaf and had no ear for French

she once burned her partner in bid whist
for making a mistake
but she would wait on a corner at night
for a guy with a suit and briefcase
who didn't want to be seen with her in the day

he wanted to buy me a Bentley
because he didn't want to be black
i wanted her to get him in the kitchen
prove she wasn't so deaf
she couldn't hear the dirt flying
but she was smarter than me
and graduated early and left town

my friend the child prodigy
always looked to me like Billie Holiday
the genius from southeast DC
told me she was a junkie
with the wrong class of friends
so was Billie Holiday she would point out

and so were the kids at the Rock Lounge
they'd never heard of Anacostia
or cared why the singer was missing some teeth
i wondered why they played reggae
when their rock 'n' roll made the punks so crazy
wondered why they didn't just get them in the kitchen
while they had them
slam dancing each other to the floor

the punks jumped on the stage
and dove into their friends

let their chains beat their thighs and arms
the crowd thought death
in two-minute intervals
heavy metal duos and creaming murder

the band of twelve-year-old rockers
wished they could do it
come like that on the refuse
of somebody's else youth

Good Friday

Blood on the pearly flesh hanging in the sun, the whole body of God, weighing down on one nail. Sighing they sang it in the convent. The pain no one could bear. Those nails, arms dead like not there, a swan, a gull, limp on a beach. The ribs falling off into smooth loins, his leanness sinking, effete like a great cat. Intricate feet, artful, torn, torn by a nail into this tree. Streams of blood on the near-white

sand. Pale fleshy curves of sea-edges, a beach. A red sash cuts across the yellowed-white uniform, the weary gold braid and buttons. Tomás's handsome gun. At the front of his weapon is a dagger for the most quiet deaths. The Padre's hand reaches into the sea—the foamy green water becomes clear in his bowl, splashes like baubles on the indians' faces. Tawny frown, black hair flashing slick. Splashes and drips the clear water to each head, *et Nomine Patria, et Fili et Spiritu Santu,* 20 times, Father, Son, Holy Ghost

Madre de Dios, rosa mystica. His gun is dusty and oily, the blade dully grey in this light. The Padre's hand makes a cross, Tomás puts the powder in, makes the cross 20 times, he shoots. 20 times. Father, we commend these souls to You. A drop of blood.

Rain. Drops of blood against the fleshy sand. Tomás thinks of the little angels of the Assumption, a delivery to heaven, his grandmother's heavy black dresses and filigree crosses, Etnairis's hungry love, her fear of falling plates, open jars, and hanging clothes when someone dies. It's a long trip home. Tomás thinks he will fuck his wife when he gets there.

Only near-white. It was old linen. Everything in the room was old. Gabrielle did not know what to make of this blood on the sheet; it was thin like a painting someone ruined in anger. It went everywhere in strokes and folds.

On the chair her gown from the dance, a feverish pink, tiny sequin straps, the orchid for her breast too deeply purple. In this room the drapes were worn and sickly, all rosiness gone next to her dress, her long clean white gloves, and silk shoes.

Gabrielle naked and spread like wet sea-brush all over a shoreline after rain runs her hands inside herself, wipes blood across her thigh. It was something Sylvain had not mentioned.

He had said so much about virgins but not blood. A sliver of pain, a small slice of pain in a tight embrace. It will feel so good he said. He said how he knew so many virgins, a point of pride with him. But this blood on the sheet—he was not a Catholic, that was his problem. That's why he didn't say. But this blood like a madwoman's hair painting the sheet was hers and the sin too was hers. Was her sin greater than his sin? If the red mystery of Mary was true then yes she was condemned. This love, this deception. Sylvain was an angel of death. This blood was the sign.

The feet of Christ, intricate, artful, belonged to an animal who could travel any terrain. The roughness sustained all rocks, dirt, undergrowth and wetness. Marguerite thought this every time she saw the paintings.

She painted in deep blues, aqua blues, pale gull whites, poinsettia red. The Christs always made her think of large elegant cats and these nails, the pain no one could bear. The suffering male cat.

The sisters sighed as they sang in Latin of the wounds of the Lamb. She remembered these guileless women all married to the wounded flesh but she painted Christs and cats: long lean leopards, cougars, panthers, jaguars, dim blue eyes like asian nights going out. Stretched out blind in deep forest floors, their bellies open to harm, ears lulled to bird calls.

In Marguerite's house crude frontier crosses were nailed together all over the floor. She had to step over them but wanted to imagine the trees — they were cut from straight trees — and the dirt and broken splinters where they were dragged. Lush flowers grew green and ivory around her crosses, filigree. His face always looked dimly like blinded by sun and narcotics on a sky caribbean green, patches of blue.

Mary escaped her. Never had a face. This pureness to fathers and sons, just a cloak hanging on a well-drafted figure, to the side or from the back. Washing the feet of Christ, Mary Mother of God, Mary Magdalene, unholy, not of God, she couldn't distinguish. A woman's body with no face.

She looked at the man God. Mary wept. The cat, its pearly underbelly exposed. Nails holding all the weight, the arms with no feeling, the face knowing eternity, drops of blood that were herself, dying there in the sun.

geography

north of the last place, west of the first

the passage made us ancient
the oldest people on earth
down in the bottom as we were
hearing the ocean heaving us
across her body
our sounds meaningless
squeals of fallen trees
without ancestors or children
all youth died
perhaps we too
crossed wrong at some cross way
days pass with meanness
we are going perhaps
but nowhere
we know about
                *
four horses flew over the sea
we lay packed below
we could hear the horses jeering
the sailors said they came for us
they came for heathens
at first we thought this must be so
some of us went
even with the chains
we looked for signs
                *
but the horses never left
their yowls and thunders
made the sailors noisy
the passage made us ancient
pirates plague all our lands
even while stealing us
where we're from and where we go
we all came alone on the boats
the passage made us ancient
each one a village, each one
all time gone

each one a tongue, a drum
a whole land

    *

i am my hunting grounds, my people's fields
and fishing villages, all that was
before the forts were built
the secret pens were shut
i am a delta, south of the gold
away from the desert east
north of the free zone
where no pirates could bring guns
Nzinga's land
the fiercest queen kept them out
north and south they waited
for her ground and minerals

    *

the new world had it's own north and south
we had to find our feet, check our limbs
how they move without getting us away
we are going perhaps
but nowhere
we know about
we went through towns with names
like Spilled Blood and Hialeah
cut through Waycross,
Vicksburg and Biloxi
north of the last place
west of the first
El Paso, Beaufort, Wilmington
died there too
we carried High John in our shoes
on the Chisholm Trail, past Salt Lake
dragging through our brothers' bodies
on the battlefields of the republic
everywhere folks said
it was like Revelations
what we should see
come the day

said the worst came first
then everything would be new
*
places without ancestors
only youth & unknown dangers
we were not going there
Babylon and Bethlehem were just towns
like the New Hopes, New Ports
and New Markets
we set up shop
invented soft-shoes and cakewalks
met secretly in New Berlin
forged gates in New London
took over New York and New Orleans
all these new places
where the talk was just talk
about freedom
we were not going there
when we found out just where we were
building it, cleaning it,
hoeing it, towing it,
even singing over it
we were going perhaps
but not there
*
our destination became a deep river
on the other side of the tracks
a gal named Sal, Treemonisha or Aretha
a fellow named My Guy
our place jumped at Woodside
raised up out of churches
and the ways of folks
named Malcolm and Fannie
each one a village, each one
all time gone
each one a tongue, a drum,
a whole land
a reason to live

those horses do not hound our strut
in the new place
old as we have become
we are going

Susannah

(*Time of the Gingham Rooster,*
collage by Romare Bearden)

that constant Susannah
bathing in her galvanized tub

the red chair sits
waiting one leg forward
like an arrogant steed
waiting for Susannah
to claim her checkered cloth

Susannah love of so many
lover of so few
no one knew their names
or saw her that way

the blue close of day
hoped she'd never succumb
never cover herself
in that black and red interior
the weary man waits for his supper
sister stands prim and expectant
this black and white rooster
coin curves and guinea hen wings
keeps his feet crossed, a prancer
poised for his portrait
as a creature of style
　　　*
that constant Susannah
bathes gleaming brown
taut and curved
in the forest
lean race horse limbs
among sparrows, wild zinnias,
tree barks mottled and smooth

that constant Susannah
under a full yellow moon
desirous and staring
at her possibility
as a goddess
or a woman with long gloves
and dark hat

a veil crosses her view
of herself and the blueness
of this brook occurs to her
as the lover she held
when a good song came

she hadn't known him
was always the same one
when blues were played
and women hummed
how good loving was

they had a way of staring at the land
smiling at light and shadow
and god's way with trees
that constant Susannah
bathing in her galvanized tub

C.T.'s variation

some springs the mississippi rose up so high
it drowned the sound of singing and escape
that sound of jazz from back
boarded shanties by railroad tracks
visionary women letting pigeons loose
on unsettled skies
was drowned by the quiet ballad of natural disaster
some springs song was sweeter even so
sudden cracks split the sky / for only a second
lighting us in a kind of laughter
as we rolled around quilted histories
extended our arms and cries to the rain
that kept us soft together

some springs the mississippi rose up so high
it drowned the sound of singing and escape
church sisters prayed and rinsed
the brown dinge tinting linens
thanked the trees for breeze
and the greenness sticking to the windows
the sound of jazz from back
boarded shanties by railroad tracks
visionary women letting pigeons loose
on unsettled skies
some springs song was sweeter even so

Mecca Flats 1907

on this landscape
like thin air
hard to breathe
behind God's back
i see the doors
but few can enter
soot flakes crowd the view
down narrow jagged streets
women's eyes peer
out windows, porches
watching for passers-by
piano playing it: C A D# E
i went up there
went to the southside
of a town wide open
that grips you like a vice
on this landscape like thin air
i see the doors
i want to enter
honky-tonk and barrelhouse
sweet relief
behind God's back
where few are so many
and the talk is loud
where love might be this old friend
sportin' in the door
take me to the southside
of anywhere that's blue
put me near the ones and nines
the five'll get you two
i like the way the hips curve
and the shirt looks new
he could bring it over here
piano playing it: C A D# E
inside this landscape
the back of Mecca Flats
the southside of anywhere
that's blue

skinny-dippin'

skinny-dippin' in the gene pool

the streets of hell are also paved
with fear of contagion
I have been swimming
in enough barbed-wire waters to know
you're not even safe on the beach
it's not just your "body fluids"
it's the grime of your skin
those dirty things you think

they are cleaning up the world again
I can see the inflammation
heartbreak & hunger scurry like hounds
even chemicals are hunting me down
on the road to Damascus
I want to be blinded like Saul
for the sake of vision
not just cause I can't take it anymore

are we talking burnt out here?
burnt out is a reason for infection
I hope I get the whole disease
I am glad to be a speck / a piece of dirt
the dark side of the earth
they're trying to clean
I want to get in their pores
want them to sweat my filth
the way a wound hurts before the dope
but then come the murderers on the road
are we talking burnt out?
they go in the camps looking for you
cause you are hiding the sores
you could be contagious
after all in the postapocalypse movies
you don't even exist

your survival is not required
for history or hollywood
in the movie *Road Warrior*

everyone is antisocial on purpose
human ties are burnt out
& human intercourse is fatiguing & dangerous
gratefully no one is traumatized anymore
& unfortunately no one goes to school

in the movie *Blade Runner*
almost everyone lives 90 stories below
almost no one else
everyone is antisocial by accident
due to overcrowding in L.A. but no one minds
& there are still parties to go to

everyone white is "off-world" more or less
everyone 90 stories down is polymorphous colored
more or less
no one has attended school in decades
in both films everyone dresses with panache
which preserves their identities
to audiences who know
there is no grounds for identity
postworld

personally I prefer the people in *Titanic*
even though they got their minds blown
when the unbelievable happened
they still believed in life
they were not burnt out
& had grounds for clinging
to lifeboats and a certain
stylish way of dressing

they could not imagine Jim Jensen
intoning without horror
that the body count goes on
that no one needs the news to know
what's going on
Beirut is one of the low levels

Dante went on about
available in ordinary life

see the corpses if you will
believe at the risk
you may see it everywhere
every body spreads infection
unless you burn it out
eyewitness news invites you
to wait for the coverage
because Jim Jensen is there
& history is in the making or
you can come skinny-dip
in my gene pool

the massacres were arbitrary
when my people were hunted down
the deaths still go on
stretching over centuries
of shades of brown
baptist, moslem,
mothers, children, fathers
burnt out of homes but living

I am not that desperate
to be numb & dumb
I'm walking 90 stories down
I know I survive
in some wretched moments
of what men do
but I am not that desperate
I don't give a shit if this is history
in the making
it should stop

I am still alive
I am still happy to be the dirt
that can't be cleaned up

scorch my earth & I will grow
from history up
under the feet of the present
burnt out is for the movies
in which we don't exist

playing the
changes

backstage drama

for Miami

They all like to hang out.
Thinking is all rather grim to them.
Snake and Minnie,
who love each other dearly,
drink in different bars,
ride home in separate cars.
They like to kiss good night
with unexplored lips.
They go out of town
to see each other open.
This they do for no one else.
Minnie does it all for God.
Snake does it all for fame.
Backstage is where they play their games;
that's why i know their business.

I was gonna talk about a race riot.
They say they've never played that town.
Fleece tells me he's seen an old movie
about a black town attacking a white one.
Sidney Poitier was the young doctor,
accused, abused and enraged.
There were Ossie Davis and Woody Strode,
Ruby Dee and a hundred unknowns.
Also Sapphire's mama as a maid.
"What was Sapphire's mama's name?" says Inez.
I was going to talk about a race riot
but we were stuck on Kingfish's mother-in-law.
Minnie kisses Snake so he'll forget about that
and I say, "They're mad, they're on the bottom
going down, stung by white justice in a white town,
and then there's other colored people,
who don't necessarily think they're colored people,
leaving them the ground."

"That's just like the dreads, the Coptics,
and the Man-ley-ites," one drunk says too loud,
"I and I know," say he.
Snake yells, "Are you crazy? No, it ain't,
and no, we don't."
"That's just like Angola," Terri chimes,
"Sometimes it's not who but what,
sometimes not what but who."

I'm trying to talk to these people
about this race riot,
someone is walking on the bar,
and every one of us belongs even now to Miami,
to people we have never seen.

Pookie and Omar want to know what's goin' on.
They always do,
'cause they're always in the bathroom
when it's goin' on.
They do everything together and not for God,
and not for fame, but for love.
At least that's what their records say.
They are a singing group that's had 13 Pookies.

Omar asks me, "What do you want to say?"
Inez interupts, "She don't know what to say,
she just wants to say something,
I understand that."
The 13th Pookie chirps, "This race riot sounds like
all the other race riots."
Fleece says, "And you sound like
12 other Pookies, Pookie."

I am still trying to talk about this race riot.
Minnie looks up and says, "We don't have anywhere
to put any more dead."
Snake puts on his coat to leave alone,
"We never did, we never did."

hunger

carnivores eat all kinds of meat
flesh that used to fly, swim, crawl
stalk & run
the limbs & moving parts
even wings & fins
some eat the skin with special relish
some the brains for luck or smarts
carnivores eat flesh
porous muscle, gristle & bone
they eat the insides of familiar bodies

the attack could not be seen by night

this little phase
keeps on the same way
without variety
jazz and compromise
making blue snow grow at the windows
mohair fumes clog my throat like cats
flames pounce without burning
shadows gather in parkas at my back
turn so i can see your face
stand where i can see you man
should someone phone
i will tell whoever it is
i cannot escape this night
even saxophones do not dry
light the brown sweat
terror in white doorways
under multicolored covers
there is no way to sleep
with the phone
falling off the hook
the blaring beep of warnings
do not leave your house
do not stay home
this is the contradiction
of when i live
even fanfares and flourishes
do not announce a truce
with our personal assailants
without variety blue dust
blood traces in floor wax
black fog and nappy lint
colorless wax spreads broad
tears across all the windows
some permanent weather
happened to this building
some misplaced coal mine
had its disaster here
and i am alive inside

so long sugar suite

actually i do love you
where i've been
where you have to ask
how someone who saw the scars
could just up and gone
the marks you cut there yourself
in place of talk
        *
your body screams for people
who will not clutch
when men can't love
haven't loved
since their first love
they call the ones they know
who love them the most
never the ones who won't admit
        *
so i gave you up
let you float out there
where asking comes from pain
on the curb under the window
your cathouse on the avenue
        *
on the fat street
severed arms fly by me
a story streams
the dialogue runs
"but i didn't have no dope"
he kept saying
"give it to me bitch
give it to me bitch
i know you got it"
        *
on the fat street
where stevie got his
all-night soul food
no one can catch a cab
on the fat street

i could just walk
back to your place
  *
but i took my chances
and gave you up
i will not say i love you
it might turn into art or an excuse
something that sounds like something
to make it seem like something
i say nothing like a lie
so i can have you
when they've all done you
and you know you have to ask
  *
what i need
to get off this
fast fat avenue
is a yellow cab
actually i do love you
but all i need to leave
to save what i have
is a yellow cab
the only threat in town

it's all in who you know, my dear

all this narcissism & silken decay
makes bleak history
& light literary gossip
having lived laughing at old taboos
they found, yes, there are others
lower, viler, more exotic
invented, if necessary
had, if they sound good
when one lives in absolutes
everything can be bought & consumed
corruption can be gradual or sudden
but it is always final
if you've seen it, you've seen it
it informs you or plagues you
or lies dormant for you later
maybe you'll get reviewed
        *
they amused themselves with their torments
even sold them in the markets
then tortured each other with flattery
after all flattery was all that was left
when personal statements were replaced
with good looks & fine wine
they hired armies to decipher their dreams

55 w.p.m.

i will not be a typist in the war
my left hand shakes
will not hold coffee
still without spilling i sing
an anthem for Bob Marley
so tired the war they prepare
with machines we need jobs
i have my work cut out
just to stay home
while you all think it's not going on
word processors and word sayers
and even legislators
are trying to say it to you just right
even kissinger admits
handling the public
is not easy
being handled is not easy either
and being in the public
is learning to say no
i will not be a typist in the war
i will win no medals
for processing the words
for the word sayers
and invoice writers
the body counters
and report makers
those "affects" that "impacted"
on the "targeted"
i have been in the public
being handled
long enough to know
i am not too old
most people are my age
i am not the wrong sex
only a few people are
i am not handicapped
in spite of my claims

i am not just too dumb
not dumb enough
not to know
i don't know what's going on
i did not call this war party to order
my left hand shakes
will not hold coffee
no, i will not be a typist in the war

in the fire lane

we are deadly decadent anarchists
living in the fire lane
you know that
we do not secure the lives
we mean to lead

because we are narcissists
I use us
because loss is personal
we don't even watch or listen
for the news
we are moving fast
we like the pleasures
the facts suggest knowing
abandonment

we are deadly in our way
the way we forget, fall asleep
fall out, leave the door open
the men with unhealed wounds
jump us, try to maim us
without even taking the bread
without even, as Wesley says,
anything "motivational"

this happened to me
and someone known to me
on the same night
have we been listening
did we hear the scream in the hall
or Ntozake say, "every three minutes"
did i know the woman
who met the mugger
on the same night
was shot for saying no
like i did

he took my head
in his hands

and bashed it to the wall
"yes, that's right, bitch"
smacked off my glasses
his brass ring cut its way
through my mouth to the gum
moved my teeth
"i'm gonna kill you"

i thought i was a doll
with a porcelain face
shattering off

i screamed
i die my way
a kick to the groin
i screamed six flights

too late but they came
he ran 'cause they came yelling
in T-shirts and drawers
canes and switchblades
the woman across the hall
barefoot with kitchen knife
and a new lover behind her

but some of us just wait
for the song to be gone
feeling taken by force
we are decadent, yes
because we know
have sat through terror
outside a window

we cannot do this fast enough
no time to write the poem
just time to say
we have got to be safe
we cannot afford the oblivion
we talk so much about

if i'm not there
you could be gone
if you don't save me
i could be lost
we have to do
here living in the fire lane
where it all moves fast
the emergency is ongoing

the song will have to
have the passion
we dispense instead of dreams
the song will have to mean
having somewhere to go
and the freedom
to move up the street
that goes there

being alone

being alone when someone loves you
is about the same
as being alone when no one does
you keep wondering where "they" are
with all this love

being alone when someone loves you is more mental
at night you try to make the knowledge of this love
show itself in the room and warm you
watching the late night movie is much easier
than being alone when someone loves you
you can turn the tv off just before it's over
and waltz yourself to sleep with your own ending

being alone when someone loves you and is far away
is like how it feels when you watch the movie to the end
and the prayer comes on
to remind you that you are sitting up alone
at a ridiculous hour of the night

being alone when someone loves you and is far away
and hasn't called or written
makes you long for the good old days
those days when you knew no one loved you
but someone one day would
yes those old days when you couldn't even imagine
this person's face
and you had nobody to be mad at about it
and you knew you would fade into forever
like the late night movie
and they'd never go away
but if they ever did have to go away
the love would keep you and
they'd write and call to remind you
and you'd sleep with a smile
instead of all these pillows and novels
and kleenex and cigarettes

some choices are just compulsions

for John Woo

it started to rain
on our bench
and in the fountain
we had half a bottle to go
we sat under the eaves
the opera, a monument
a height from which a woman
had been dropped
i could see it was a long way
for a body to fall
still breathing or not
"this is just a poem to you,
my life, all the things i say,
you use it all—
it's all for a poem, isn't it?"
it never stopped raining
i was surprised and so was he
i soon admitted
my work is where i put it
i love that he told me
i burn out everything
this kind of vandal / thief
what i have become
"it's all the work," he said
like i have no morals
sometimes i see it, catch me
stealing my own anger
in the middle of a fight
chooses productivity
who used to pay her money
get on the roller coaster

and burn it out
just to burn it out
be blinded
scream burn it out
get a rush
pay the money
ride again
maybe find a partner
for the thrill
i could scream
the rest of my life
or watch you
and feel that
at my work
i burn it out

bicameral brain

for Olga & June

had in mind the two-faced kind
staring from time to time at one another
or passing bits of sense across
started out as one smooth body
with not much to go on
feeding, hugging & gazing out
the world close by
parted as they began to see further
caress and feast on their own
slowly tore easily day by day
split of necessity into perfection
more than some parts
 or echoing chambers
two whole creatures
held together by the involuntary
sharing of each electric instant

there is no one out there

for Renee

the little girl drew fire
no one could see it was flame
all it was
like blood slipping from a cut
just what it was
the fact of blood
an illusion that was fact
like pain
hurt but left no scar
　　　*
someone said it wasn't pretty
her flame
consumed the page
　　　*
there is no one out there
they tell me
i believe them
whoever they are
striking matches in my dark
　　　*
the woman was a fire
no one could see she was flame
all she was
the fact of herself
consuming air to burn
　　　*
there is no one out there
there is no out there
no pretty, no pain
i'm telling me

the adults who needed help from the baby (Louise)

of course, at the last minute she said
she wouldn't go through with it
this made me laugh and reminded me
Georgia is a rebellious person
she thought she would stay like she was
but what she was was the irrevocable you

we were *all* mixed up
many of us thought *she* was doing it
some others thought they were doing it
and did it on her day to do it
some of us wished we were doing it
or decided we could help her do it
if we just invited her to lunch
no one was doing anything
only having the dreams babies induce
like labor in the middle of the night
we sit up and say, "the baby is coming"
and we don't know what we're talking about
i said it in the middle of the dishes
"let me call her and see if she's doing it"

we were *all* mixed up
assigning names from goddesses and gods
the living and the dead, the true, the brave
people we imagine in our lives or selves
you might've been a Walter or Satchmo, you know
if somebody else was doing it
but then Satchmo was really Gabriel
which would have made you Gabrielle
in fact, if you were a novel by Gabriel García Márquez
this would all be because of the weather

the warm winter we had our worst blizzard
Georgia was afraid of ice
and wore the neighbor's boots
and the sweater that belonged to Bob
which I call mine

part of the all-night-shift wardrobe
days when people did funny things
with paper called repro
and pens called nonrepro

your name would have been Buendía, good day
and a female ending would be very important
Importante Buendía
the last day of February it was oddly balmy
people in the town cracked their windows
in spite of slush from snow some weeks ago
a fog of delirium crept in all the kitchens
gossiping took over everyone who'd had the dreams
"oh, the baby came already?"
"oh, the baby finally came?"
"the baby came when i said she would."

a fireplace still puffs on the next street
a trumpet player comes in from the rain
his name begins with an L
he asks for a J and begins to play
i'm in the pool i keep by my typewriter
it's swimming-pool blue, of course
and light makes grey phantoms on the water
but i have my goggles
and a pretty wide smile
this could go on for a hundred buendías
it's still all up in the air
who you are
thank god pushing yourself headlong
at last into the confusion

potholes

love for you decays
like new york streets
falls short
like heat inspectors
and water supplies
the longer i say here
the less i even like you
my ceiling gives out
a little each night
and i think of you
little crashes
like birds with bad wings
wake me up
to a certain bitter desire
for radio, credit or a car
i could get out of new york
with the proper attitude
you're not that cute
and crying may be good
for the complexion
but so is oatmeal
i'm not that good at it
your love is crooked
running all in my way
leaning, falling
looking for a place to lay
new york is a hard rock
for that sort of thing
people will just turn
and walk away saying
i really don't need this
i was going uptown

as i fly over this time

for Dianne McIntyre

as i fly over this time
rising over only this
so much painted suffering
unseen grimaces and stares
among spruce greens
these few forests left
all of us trying to be alone
quiet and blind
*
i see soldiers in bus stations
with colored names
polaroid shots
their girlfriends chew gum
smile wide
*
in all this silver of sky
like stars these wheels
car gears lampshades
electrical refuse
zen oiled and greased
the believers now so many
now so tired of the sad songs
the endless yearnings for war
and more and more
*
dumb cries i sigh
trying to get out of town
i am writing on the wall
it will be painted over
like all the songs
once outside
but as i fly over this time
*
dianne is dancing
touching the far reaches

leaping and teaching
she strokes and struts the air
none of us stumbles
or fears their lives
steel beams and rail tracks
strike an E-flat, B-flat, A
E-flat, B-flat, A
dianne is dancing
no one can handle the hostages
terror is abandoned
because of light
breaking in leaves
because the center is gone
we are still breathing
and the swing is our bodies

telepathy

when in the house
something became clear
they listened to the wind
which could not be told
from the ocean

she felt the house move
like people stepping
he heard a night noise
just a sound in a new house

they loved each other anyway
late they hid together
under sheets blankets talk

they loved each other
as best they could
at any moment
something became clear

they shut up and sighed
because something true
disappointed them
made them sad
they never knew the same things

what infant wailing
on one side of the earth
he heard as himself
she thought a glass pane
creaking
always at this time

playing solitaire

for Jessica

the thing about playing solitaire
is that right from the start
you begin to draw the same cards
in spite of all the possibilities
with their backs to you

a black jack lies under the diamond queen
face to face where you can't see
you suspect them
because you dealt the cards
and what's in your hand
keeps coming up nines, sixes
they look alike
but won't lay down
spades where you need hearts or diamonds
can't get rid of that black queen

you move them around in your palm
you turn up one turn it down
turn up the other
you think if you look again
you'll see what you missed before
you'll see where they belong
sooner or later

maybe if you argue with them
or ignore the obvious moves
but after you go with red
you have to go with black

a king has to have his own spot
according to the rules
queens sit around on kings' laps

collecting jacks & other numbers
aces fly over ignoring all order
to get all the cards on the table
you have to admit
you're the only one

when i play solitaire i cheat
i am an ace
i shuffle the cards
it's not that i have to win
i just don't want to give up
and the facts i have to face
sit in the palm of my hand
vicious cycles break my heart

black spaces

for Robert Hayden

in the black and few spaces
i find my fire
to make my own
meet the marauders
where they live and die
in the black and few spaces
where human recall comes strong
like bars of peace be still
there prophets are common folk
who live among neighbors
and eat friendly bread
in the black and few spaces
where i can listen to you
we all have lovers
bodies leave impressions
yes, there are still sacred spaces
dance moving through them
in the black and few spaces
i can hear myself singing
songs only some of us know
truth only some of us believe
laughs not everyone can laugh
the blackness of it makes me grin
so i could die for you
in the black and few spaces
i find my fire
to make my own
i find my fire
to keep my own